©1976/2010 Sanrio Co., Ltd
978-0-00-736507-4
1 3 5 7 9 10 8 6 4 2

First published in the UK by HarperCollins Children's Books in 2010

Printed and bound in China.

Hello Kitty

Annual 2011

HarperCollins *Children's Books*

To do list

You don't have to wait for the New Year to make resolutions! There are so many exciting things I want to do, and so many people to do them with that I've made a list now. Do you have one too? If not, I hope this book will give you loads of ideas!

Things I'd love to do:

1) Take up a new sport
2) Learn a new language
3) Stay in touch with my family
4) Go on holiday with Dear Daniel
5) Revamp my wardrobe...again!
6) Learn to cook Italian food
7) Work on my poetry
8) Buy my friends fabulous birthday presents way ahead of time
9) Save up for a special treat
10) Hold a party for all my friends

Why not make your own list now?

1) Tidy up
2) Meet my friends

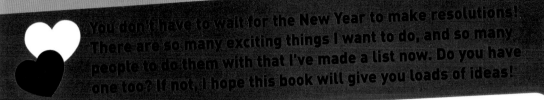

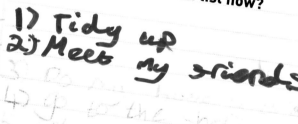

6

Welcome to my world

My world is filled with the things I love - music, fashion, crafts, my friends and my family.

I live in London. It's the best city in the world! You can never run out of things to do, not to mention great places to eat, and, of course, shop!

I like all kinds of music, whether I'm listening to my MP3 player or writing my own songs on my guitar.

Although I have lots of hobbies, sewing is one of my favourites. I work on complex projects, like creating funky clothes from scratch, as well as simple projects, like finding vintage clothes in charity shops and adding some detail to create a brand new look.

My favourite places in London:

1) Portobello Market - a fantastic place to shop for vintage and fashionable clothes
2) The London Eye - what a view!
3) Hyde Park on a sunny day
4) Leicester Square - packed full of cinemas!

As well as Mama and Papa, I have a twin sister called Mimmy. Having a sister your own age is fantastic for all sorts of reasons. For one thing, it doubles the size of your wardrobe!

My boyfriend is called Dear Daniel. He's one of my best friends, and I don't know what I'd do without him. We've been going out for a while now, and I love him more every day.

I'm lucky enough to have lots of friends, and we really know how to have fun. Last winter, we made a snowman and went skating on the ice rink.

Shoes, Shoes, Shoes!

Are shoes a girl's best friend? I certainly think so! I have so many pairs I can't count them all. Here are some of my favourite styles that I think every girl should have:

Boots

What's your style? Ankle, calf or knee high? Whichever you prefer, boots are perfect for winter months and look great with skirts, dresses or jeans. They never go out of fashion!

Sandals

My favourite style of footwear! Elegant and classic, they glam up any outfit and make your legs look lusciously long!

Folding

These are so convenient to pop into your bag! You can fold them in half and they have an elastic opening that stretches to fit comfortably round your foot!

Flats

Aah, so comfy. Flats are an ideal day shoe. If I know I'll be walking around a lot I always wear my cutest pink ballet pumps, either with tights and a skirt or with jeans.

Courts

Court shoes are very versatile and come in a variety of styles suitable for both smart daywear and glam eveningwear. Whether platform, patent or peep-toe, there's a style to suit everyone.

Party feet

Every fashionista should own at least one pair of heels, but as every girl knows, wearing high heels can leave your feet feeling extremely sore! So here are my tips to minimise discomfort and leave you free to enjoy your special shoes on those special occasions:

★ Don't buy heels that are ridiculously high, no matter how much you love them! If you know you won't be able to walk in them, it's best not to waste your money. Be realistic!

★ If you're wearing a new pair of high heels for the first time, make sure you take a few plasters with you in your bag. Shoes can rub your feet in a number of different places: the back of your heel and the tops of your toes are the real killers! If you start to feel a sting, pop into the nearest bathroom and apply plasters to the affected areas. This will soothe the sting and protect your skin from further friction.

★ Most chemists and shoe shops stock a fantastic range of gel cushions which help reduce the aching in the balls of your feet. And at very reasonable prices every party girl can afford them!

★ If your bag is big enough, pop a pair of flats in for the trip home. Failing that, try to sit down occasionally to take the weight off your feet.

★ If you still find your feet a little worse for wear at the end of the night, give them a good soak when you get in. I like to sit back and listen to some relaxing music with my feet in a bowl of warm water and soothing foot oil. Mmm, bliss!

Shoe care

It's important to look after your shoes. I have a shoe rack next to my wardrobe - it stops my shoes from getting damaged in the bottom of the wardrobe, and displays them clearly so I can see exactly what I have. I have so many pairs of shoes I'm sure I'd forget about some if I didn't have them right in front of me!

Love is in the air

I love Dear Daniel, and we try to do special, thoughtful things for each other. Sometimes we go out for a posh meal, but that can be expensive, and we both know that the most romantic presents are the ones that come from your heart, not your purse!

How do you know when you're in love?

* When just thinking of him makes you smile
* When you'd rather stay at home with him than go out with anyone else
* When you miss him as soon as he's gone
* When he lets you borrow his clothes!

Things I love about Dear Daniel:

1. His cute fluffy hair.

2. His dynamic approach to life.

3. His super-smooth style.

4. How romantic he is.

5. Everything!

12

Here are some of the things we like to do:

* Go for a romantic walk, hand in hand.
* Take a rickshaw ride around London.
* Go out for a meal - or cook it ourselves!
* Write love notes for each other and hide them in special places.

Showing you care

If you've got a special talent, why not try to create something for the one you love?

Making presents for Dear Daniel makes me feel all warm and fuzzy inside! Every year I bake Valentine's cookies for him, and I design cards for his birthday and other special occasions. At the moment I'm writing a song about him, but that's taking time because I want to get it just right.

What do you do for your boyfriend or special crush?

My FacePlace page

I love keeping in touch with my friends online, and there are so many social networking sites to choose from these days that I'm spoilt for choice. Here's a screenshot of my page on FacePlace.

FacePlace

You have 1 new message from **Dear Daniel**.

Interests:

Fashion, music, photography, creative writing, travel, cooking, my friends

Invitations: 2

Tim and **Tammy** invite you to their party on Wednesday

Tracy invites you to join her FacePlace group, I Love Learning to Play Guitar

Blog:

Saturday February 26th:
'Off skating' Cold today so I wrapped up warm in my cosy scarf and went to meet everyone at the ice rink. We had such fun! I'm getting really good and can glide along on one...

Archive entries:

Thursday February 24th:
'Girls' night in'
Monday February 21st:
'Helping Papa'
Friday February 18th:
'Baked the yummiest cookies today at baking club'

Friends:

Tippy says: Hello Kitty came for a visit yesterday and we...;

Jody says: I've lost my blue hat, did I leave it at anyone's house?

Events:

Hello Kitty, you may be interested in the vintage fashion show in London's West End on Saturday March 5th.

Do you blog? If you're the creative type, it can be a fantastic way of practising your writing or showing off your latest drawings and designs. The only problem I have is that sometimes it's hard to think of exactly what to write! If you get stuck, why not flick through this book and see if it inspires you?

Blog tips:

★ Blog at least once a week to keep your site fresh.
★ If you comment on other people's blogs too, they'll take an interest in yours.
★ If you write anything very personal, don't forget to put it under a privacy lock.

Makeover and mend

Spring is the perfect season for a wardrobe makeover. You don't have to spend much to give all sorts of old clothes a fresh new look. You can update things you already own or shop for some vintage bargains that can be adapted to fit your style.

Younger Hello Kitty fans should ask a grown-up for help with sewing.

Here are some of my favourite ways to revamp old clothes:

If a garment is damaged or torn, cover the holes by sewing on buttons or beads. Lace can cover a worn-looking seam, and will add a bohemian touch.

Spilled coffee down your white shirt? Simply dye it black and go goth!

Customising an outfit will mean it's a one-off - exclusively your style - and it's so easy to do! If you're not confident at sewing, accessories like satin ribbon can be applied to clothes with special fabric tape.

Try car boot sales and charity shops for cool vintage items that you can customise - cheap and chic!

Change the buttons on last season's coat for some funky new ones of a different colour or shape.

Even shoes can be glammed up. Add some glitter to worn-looking leather and you've got yourself a trendy new look!

Hold a swap party with friends, to share unwanted clothes, and maybe pick up some gems yourself. You should see the fabulous puffball skirt that I got last week!

An old top can be turned into a beach bag by sewing up the bottom edge and applying funky accessories like ribbon and beads.

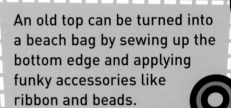

A hat is the perfect stylish accessory for any outfit. Try picking up a plain one in a charity shop or on the high street and adding your own funky accessories.

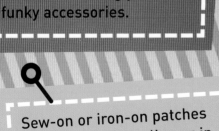

Sew-on or iron-on patches are easy to find online or in your local high street. You can get anything from cute baby animals to your favourite TV characters.

What's your fashion-diva style?

I love dressing up in chic new outfits, and following the latest trends worn by my favourite fashionistas! Take this quiz to check out your own style:

1) You are invited to a last-minute party. What do you decide to wear?
a) Skinny jeans with a black top, and lots and lots of jewellery.
b) A little black dress and heels - sophistication is your middle name!
c) A unique vintage number that no-one else will have.
d) A floral dress and leggings, you know it looks good and will fit in with what the other girls are wearing.

2) You head to the shops with your friends. Where's the first place you visit?
a) Accessorize - you're treating yourself to a funky new bag.
b) Selfridges - to grab those new Prada shoes you've had your eye on for ages.
c) The local boutique - hidden away but where you're sure to pick up a one-off.
d) Topshop - you're guaranteed to find a super stylish outfit!

3) It's your birthday. What does your friend buy you as the perfect present?
a) Earrings and a matching necklace.
b) A Chanel purse - it cost a lot but she knows you will love it!
c) A customised T-shirt that she has made for you.
d) A skirt you saw in your favourite fashion magazine last week.

4) You are shopping for a new pair of shoes. What style do you go for?
a) Sparkly high heels - a great way to accessorise a party dress.
b) You don't mind as long as they have a designer label.
c) Bright red lace-ups - will definitely be a head-turner.
d) Cute ballet pumps which look good with everything.

5) Which fashion item could you not live without?
a) Scarves - great for brightening up an outfit.
b) Sunglasses - you always like feeling glamorous!
c) Your faux-fur jacket from the charity shop - it's one of a kind.
d) Your favourite pair of jeans - perfect for all occasions!

Mostly as

You are a Decorations Diva! You love accessorising your clothes with matching items, and lots of them. Jewellery, scarves, and cute hair bows are a fun and cheap way to liven up an old outfit, and as I always say, you can never have too many accessories!

Mostly bs

You are a Designer Diva! There's nothing you love more than splashing out on gear created by the biggest and the best fashion designers in the world. For you, price is perfection, but don't be afraid to look elsewhere. High-street fashion can look just as fab, but will save you pennies in the long run - so you can buy twice the amount of clothes!

Mostly cs

You are a Daring Diva! You don't follow the trend - you set your own! People are jealous of your creativity and individual look, which usually comes from vintage styles you have customised. People always come to you for advice on where to find the most unique fashion.

Mostly ds

You are a Trend-grabbing Diva! Look out Vogue, here comes the most fashionable girl around! You are always up to date with the latest trends, and love nothing more than flicking through magazines to find the newest look. Don't be afraid to try something different though, you don't want to end up being the same as everyone else!

What does music say about you?

I don't know about you, but I love singing along to my favourite tunes! But did you know that the type of music you love says a lot about who you are? Take this music quiz and see what your favourite songs say about you:

1) You're deciding on that all-important outfit for tomorrow night's concert. What look do you go for?
a) Your favourite dress - you want to look (and sound) the part.
b) Something sparkly but comfy too - you're planning on dancing the night away!
c) Easy! Jeans and a black T-shirt with the name of the band on the front.

2) You arrive at the gig just as it's starting. What's the first thing you do?
a) Sing your heart out - it's your all time favourite song!
b) Join in with the dance routine.
c) Crowd surf!

3) Your bedroom walls are covered in posters of:
a) The winner from the last K-Factor.
b) Your favourite boy-band.
c) That famous guitar player.

4) Your dream job in the music biz would be:
a) A scary judge on a top talent show.
b) A choreographer for a new girl group.
c) A tour manager - think of the travel!

5) Your favourite music-related activity is:
a) Karaoke night with the girls.
b) Copying superstar dance routines from the music channels.
c) Summer festivals - great music and great weather!

Mostly as

You're a Singing Sensation! There's nothing you love more than blasting out the hits from the biggest divas in the world and singing along with them. Even if you don't sound quite like them, there's nothing that will stop you from trying!

Mostly bs

You're a Disco Diva! They don't call you a dancing queen for nothing! Inspired by great dance acts, you love being the centre of attention on the dance floor, and showing off your new moves to your friends. Dancing is one of my favourite ways to have fun and keep fit at the same time!

Mostly cs

You're a Rock Chick! You are a huge fan of rock and roll, and lead the lifestyle that goes with it. You follow the alternative fashions and like your music the louder the better. You would even love to be a rock-star yourself one day!

Prom night preparations

Prom night is one of the most glamorous events in a girl's social calendar, so when yours finally arrives, you'll want to make sure you're fully prepared to party! Getting ready for your Prom, or any other special occasion, can be so much fun! It's a chance for you to look even more fabulous than usual, so you should really make the most of it, and enjoy yourself! You can use my top tips for Prom Night for all kinds of other special occasions as well.

One week before:

Plan your outfit as far in advance as possible, don't leave it to the last minute. You'll want to look really special so bear that in mind when choosing a dress, and be daring!

Once you have your dress, you can choose accessories to complement it. Choosing jewellery or a bag in a clashing colour can work really well, but you may want to stick to a specific colour theme.

In the run up to the big day, you might want to fit in as many pampering treatments as you can. Why not give yourself a full body exfoliation followed by intensive moisturiser a few days before? For your face a cleansing mask can really help your skin to look fresh. For hair, an intensive moisturising conditioner can revitalise even the dullest-looking locks.

The day of the Prom:

It's a good idea for everyone to have a relaxing shower or bath before meeting up, so that you can get straight down to the most important bits. It's best to sort out your hair first as it can be the most time-consuming part. You can go super-sleek with a good pair of hair straighteners, or if you have more time get the curling tongs out and get creative. Don't forget the hairspray and any grips or bands you might need to help secure your do in place!

If you haven't done so already, give yourself a quick mani-pedi so your hands and feet are looking fabulous too.

Give yourself two hours so that you aren't rushing. I always invite one or two close friends round to get ready with me, it's much more fun! Make sure your room (and the bathroom) are clean, and that there is space for everyone to spread out. You'll need a full-length mirror as well as a make-up mirror. Put on your favourite music to get you in the party mood and you're ready to begin.

It's a good idea when wearing a special dress to put it on before applying make-up, so you don't get anything on it if you have to pull it over your head. Be careful when pulling dresses over your head that you don't mess up your hair - it's a good idea to ask a friend to help at this stage! You can also add your jewellery now.

Make your eyes as dramatic as you dare. A shimmery eye shadow is perfect for that evening look, and don't limit yourself to your usual shade. Pick something that will really dazzle! If you have a steady hand, a dash of eyeliner will give your eyes a sophisticated edge. To finish, a coat of black mascara will give you perfectly defined peepers.

For the final glam touch, add lip balm or lip gloss, and go with a tinted gloss for maximum effect.

Go as glam as you like for Prom make-up. Start with foundation to even out your skin tone, and then dust powder over the top to give a matt finish. Add a little colour to your cheeks, but don't go too dark, especially if you are naturally pale. You can always add more.

Time for a quick pic of the group before you leave, and then you're all set! Don't forget to plan your ride to the Prom - you don't want to be walking far in such a fabulous outfit! I always ask Papa to give me a lift there and back.

23

Revamp your room

April is a great time for a spring clean. If you've been letting the dust build up on the top shelf, it might not show up in winter, but once the sun starts shining you'll be able to see everything! Cleaning isn't much fun, so I like to liven it up by giving my room a bit of a revamp at the same time. Here are some top tips to make cleaning fun:

Have a cleaning party! Your room will soon be sparkling with four or five friends vacuuming and scrubbing away alongside you and your favourite music playing. Plus you can all take turns helping each other.

Make sure you clean out the back of your wardrobe, even though you rarely see it. You want to look after your clothes, so you can't have them living against a dusty wall when you aren't wearing them - they deserve the best treatment!

If you want to give your bedroom a completely new look but don't have the budget for new stuff, moving your furniture around can make a huge difference and give it a completely different feel. If you decide to move your bed you might find it has left marks in the carpet. If it's a real problem you could buy a cheap, colourful rug to cover the marks. Or why not make one yourself?

I've framed all my favourite photos and have them up on my wall and sitting on my desk. Sometimes, when you see something every day, the fabulousness of it wears off. You don't want this to happen to your favourite photos, so rearrange them, put them in new frames or swap the photos round when you feel you need a change.

It's amazing what turns up when you're doing a really thorough clean - Christmas cards that have fallen behind bookcases, old clothes you had forgotten about, or CDs that you haven't listened to in ages. Collect everything you find and write a blog entry, make a collage or write a story about the memories they bring back.

I find it really hard to keep the area behind my computer tidy, and I'm sure you do too. There are just too many cables waiting to trip you up! I have the same problem with my TV and DVD players. You can get special cable holders to keep everything tidy, but they're often only available in boring plastic. Instead, why not hang a colourful curtain in the space under your desk, to hide all those messy trailing leads?

Snap and shoot

Here we are at the retro night!

This is me trying to wake up in the morning when we went camping!

Taking lots of photos of the things you do together is a really great way to keep friendships strong.

Having a surprise picnic with Tracy!

Jody and Fifi wore such fabulous outfits at my fancy dress party

After the fun times, the memories go on! I use photos to decorate my walls and surfaces, and also as a slideshow screensaver on my computer.

If you have the right kind of camera or phone, it's also fun to take videos of your friends. I've got a video of Dear Daniel waving and blowing a kiss so I can watch it when we can't be together. Why not record a special message that your friend or boyfriend can play back when they're sad or lonely?

If you're thinking of becoming a professional photographer, you'll need to get as much practice as possible. Why not create a portfolio of shots of your friends? You're sure to have plenty of volunteers when recruiting models!

Saving the pennies

There are so many things I want to do and there's never quite enough money for them all. That's why it's important to save for a rainy day - or for a special treat that you've planned in advance. The problem is picking which special treat to save for first! Whenever I'm tempted to spend a bit too much, I get out my wish list and think of all the great things I'm saving up for.

My Wish list

1.

The latest mobile phone

I always try to have a stylish model, not just because it's trendy, but because keeping in touch with my friends is so important. I want so many apps that my current phone can't keep up. Time for an upgrade!

2.

A new guitar

I've been improving lately, and I think I could really rock if I just had a better guitar! Still, it's not all about the equipment. Which reminds me, I must go and practise now...

3.

That designer dress

I love making fabulous outfits out of ordinary high street clothes, but sometimes you've got to splash out on something really amazing. I've got my eye on this dress!

5.

Happiness!

I know I won't get this by splashing the cash - in fact I'll feel better if I know I haven't overspent and that I have some money for emergencies. So I always leave a few pounds in my bank account, no matter how much I want to spend them.

4.

Dance lessons

Won't Dear Daniel be surprised when we go out partying and I wow him with my new moves!

6.

Skiing lessons

I'd really love to go to the indoor ski slope and have one-to-one skiing lessons. They have real snow on the slope, and there are loads of other activities to try while you're there, like snowboarding, bowling and even rock climbing. I'm planning on getting a group of friends together and spending a fun-filled weekend there!

7.

A moped - or even a car

Walking is good for you but it takes too long, and when you're wearing your favourite pair of heels it's impossible! When my friends call me up for an unexpected party, I'd love to be able to jump on my bike and scoot on round.

Note to self:
one more month of saving and I'll be able to afford a new mobile! The car might take a bit longer...

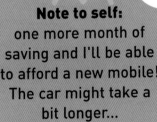

29

Great getaways

Holidays are the best part of the year! Now, what do I want to do first? Skiing or surfing, sunny beach break or a 'staycation'? Here are some pictures of holidays I've been on to inspire you:

Snow holidays

Skiing can be very exciting, especially with a group of friends. And I think coming home to a lovely warm bath afterwards is even better.

City holidays

Las Vegas is like nowhere else on Earth. Where else can you find a one-third-scale version of the Eiffel Tower, and a hotel shaped like New York skyscrapers on the same street? But my favourite place has to be the Forum Shops at Caesars. Or how about The Big Apple itself? Here's a picture I took in New York when the driver let me pose in his cab!

N.Y.C. TAXI K T

Theme parks

If you need to save money and have opted for a 'staycation', there are lots of theme parks in the country or even funfairs travelling around the UK during the summer months. The local tourist information office should be able to tell you what is visiting when.

Adventure holidays

Do you want to go white-water rafting, or deep-sea diving? I've always wanted to fly in a hot-air balloon!

Beach holidays

What could be more relaxing? Just remember to pack the sunscreen and don't fall asleep in the sun, or you'll wake up bright red and very sore, like poor Dear Daniel did last year.

Indoor games

Whee! Indoor bowling is great fun, and perfect for when the weather's miserable. Before I go on holiday, I always check there will be something to do inside if it rains.

Mani-pedi tips

Every girl loves to look her best, and what better way to pamper yourself on a budget than by giving yourself a mani-pedi at home? Your hands and feet work very hard and deserve extra special care all year round.

You will need:

- ✶ Cotton pads or balls
- ✶ Cotton buds
- ✶ Nail varnish remover
- ✶ Nail file
- ✶ Nail trimmer/ scissors
- ✶ Nail varnish
- ✶ Foot file
- ✶ Foot moisturiser
- ✶ Hand moisturiser

Tip: it's a good idea to have your cotton pads and nail varnish remover on hand in case you smudge. Soaking cotton buds in varnish remover makes tidying up edges much easier.

Pedicure

1. Starting with your feet, make sure you have removed any old varnish from your nails and that your feet are clean and dry. **2.** File your feet using your foot file to remove any hard skin. **3.** Rinse your feet, then apply moisturiser, allowing a few minutes for the moisturiser to be absorbed. This will give you beautifully soft feet.

4. If your nails are too long, cut them with your nail trimmer. It's up to you what length you keep your nails but the nail should never be longer than the toe. **5.** Next, using your nail file, shape your nails. It's best to file your nails flat across the top to reduce the risk of ingrowing toenails.

6. Before applying varnish, wipe all moisturiser residue from your nails, as it will not stick to the moisturiser.

7. You can get away with some fantastically bold colours on your feet, so be daring! I love hot pink or purple, or classic red. Working from the outside in on each foot, carefully paint each nail, but make sure you leave a small gap between the varnish and the cuticle, and the skin on either side of your nail. This will give you a neater and more professional-looking finish. **8.** Leave to dry for ten minutes, add a second coat if necessary, and you're ready to flaunt your fabulous feet in your favourite pair of open-toed shoes!

Manicure

Now for your hands. Again, make sure any old varnish has been removed and that your hands are clean and dry.

1. Apply hand moisturiser to soften your skin and leave it to absorb for a few minutes.

2. Wipe all moisturiser residue from your nails.

3. Cut your nails if they are too long, or move straight on to filing. You might choose to round your nails off at the edge or make them more square. It's up to you!

4. Some people find bold colours don't work well on their hands, but if you're not one of them then you're lucky! If you are, a classic French manicure pink suits everybody, and there are dozens of other subtle colours to choose from. Again paint from the outside in and leave a small gap between the varnish and the cuticle, and the skin around your nails. Cotton buds soaked in varnish remover are even handier when giving yourself a manicure - unless you're ambidextrous you're likely to find painting one hand more difficult than the other. If you get the shakes you could try resting the wrist of the hand you are using to paint on the edge of a surface, but make sure the surface is protected in case you drip!

5. Leave to dry for ten minutes, add a second coat or clear top coat if necessary and you're ready to party!

Travel tips

Going on a summer holiday is super fun! But it's best to plan as much as possible in advance. Here are my personal tips for making sure that everything goes swimmingly:

If you're going somewhere exotic, learn a bit about the local culture in advance. That way you'll get much more out of the trip. It's also a good idea if at least one member of the group learns a few basic phrases in the local language.

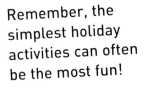

If we're staying in self-catering accommodation, I always help Mama with the cooking.

Remember, the simplest holiday activities can often be the most fun!

Take some fun games along with you in case the weather is horrible and you're stuck indoors. Make sure they're games that everyone enjoys!

Everyone in my family has different tastes, so we take it in turns to choose the day's activities.

You might want to spend some time doing your own thing. Last year Papa played golf while Mimmy and I went to the sea life centre. Great fun!

If you're holidaying with friends, make sure you know who is responsible for things like booking the tickets and planning major outings. Don't just leave it to one person, or you may end up disagreeing!

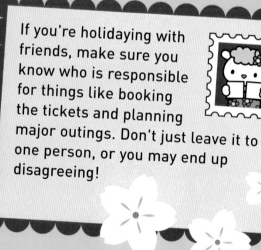

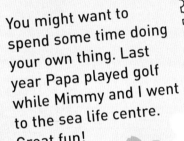

Dear Diary

My diary is one of the most important books I own. I don't know what I'd do if I lost it - probably miss all sorts of fun outings and events!

Monday 7 August

Sleepover/Makeover session with the girls.

Tuesday 8 August

Auntie's birthday, don't forget to call!

Art lesson 11am at the college. Don't forget to wear splash-proof clothes!

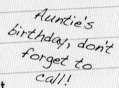

HK rocks!

Wednesday 9 August

Shopping with Fifi. Get present for Tracy.

Thursday 10 August

Tracy's birthday! Party 7pm at her house.

Friday 11 August

Country walk with Mama and Papa.

Wear in new boots before walking long distances.

Saturday 12 August

Baking with Mama. Ask her to show me how to make chocolate cheesecake!

Sunday 13 August

Picnic in the park with Dear Daniel.

hello kitty!

Poetry competition deadline tomorrow – must send entry today!

 **Diaries are fun, but you have to make sure to keep them up to date or you get hopelessly confused. When I'm rich, I think I'll hire a personal assistant to look after mine!**

The K-Factor

This year I'm entering the K-Factor talent contest. Even if I don't win, it will be a fantastic experience, and maybe I'll make some contacts in the music biz!

I'm going to play my guitar but I can't decide how to style my act. Should I play a modern tune or something more classic? And then there's the small matter of picking my outfit...

I've taken pictures of myself so I can show my friends and ask their opinion on what look to go for. What's your advice?

I love this purple and red combo!

This is a really fun look. Check out the cute shoes!

I really like my look here, maybe I should ask Fifi to join me on bass.

This style is super cool!

This outfit is really chic, and I love the stars!

What about my classic guitar and Western-themed look?

Be a fashion editor

I love being creative, so I've decided to start my own magazine. All my friends are helping out, and I hope you will too.

At any editorial meeting, it's important to brainstorm. So far we've got a few ideas for articles, but we need a lot more. Can you think of some, and try them out on the cover? Look at the covers of your favourite magazines for inspiration.

Articles for the first issue

It's a Wrap-Up: Editor Hello Kitty chooses her super styles for this autumn.

Gigs galore: Music editor Fifi on the trail of the hottest new bands.

Field Day: Sports editor Tracy looks at the latest sports apparel crazes.

Quiz: What's your style?

Themes

Each issue is going to have a theme and the first one is fashion. Next will be film, food and music. After that, who knows? Maybe an art issue? Or should we do something a bit more quirky?

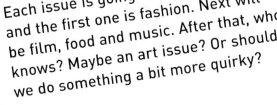

Cover plan

[Magazine title is] Style Leader
No. 1
In our first issue...

Issue 1

Here are some rough covers I have been working on...

Here is a blank cover for you to have a go...

41

Music crossword

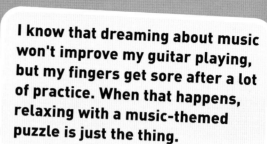

I know that dreaming about music won't improve my guitar playing, but my fingers get sore after a lot of practice. When that happens, relaxing with a music-themed puzzle is just the thing.

Clues

Across

2. Some artists are inspired by one of these, and it's also the name of a band (4)
4. The sound comes out of these at a concert (4)
5. Another word for a show or act (11)
7. Instruments you hit (5)
9. _____ n' blues is a famous musical style (6)
10. Term for a highly-strung female singer (4)
12. A metallic version of 7 across (7)
13. What a recording studio adds to the sound (10)
14. It's important to play in time with the _____ (4)
16. Another word for vocalist (6)
17. Another word for 3 down (5)

Down

1. Everyone dreams of _____ and fortune (4)
3. You can be in a rock one, or tie your hair back with an elastic one! (4)
6. A wind instrument that's used a lot in jazz. (9)
8. Everyone dreams of being a _____ (4)
11. Another word for a group, or part of a play (3)
14. A type of guitar that plays low notes (4)
15. The thing you sing into (10)
17. String instrument, popular with rock bands. (6)
18. A band needs a bus to go on _____ (4)
19. The place where you perform (5)
20. The black and white part of a piano (9)

Do you love music as much as me? My favourite bands rock my world, and I get such a buzz when I learn to play their songs myself! It's so exhilarating to turn up one of my favourite tracks and play along.

43

Be a sport

Sport keeps your body healthy and releases endorphins, so you always feel better after a good workout. We can't all be professionals, but there's no need to be shy, just have fun. I certainly do! These are just some of the sports I like to play:

Tennis

The ultimate summer game. Cute skirts, yummy orange slices, and a ball that won't knock you out if you miss it with your racket!

Golf

It's not just for old men these days! Golfing is a leisurely sport that gives you plenty of time for chatting between shots. The outfits are fabulous - with so many colours and patterns there's something for everyone. And I do love driving around in those little carts!

Running

Anyone can go running or jogging on a nice sunny day! All you need is your running shoes, a hairband and your MP3 player.

Swimming

The perfect sport for a scorching summer. Next time I'm at the seaside, I want to take proper diving lessons.

Basketball

It does help to be very tall if you want to play professionally, but there's no need for that if you just want to shoot some hoops with your friends at the local gym.

Football

Women's football is getting more and more popular. Watch out boys, I'm learning to Bend it like Beckham!

Favourite things

In winter, when it's cold and dark and miserable, I call a friend, and we chat about our favourite things. The other night, we did an A-Z. Next time you're feeling blue, why not fill in your own choices?

A is for apples.

Crunchy and yummy - and healthy.

B is for bow.

The greatest accessory. You'd never catch me without mine!

C is for cookies.

BISCUIT

Fun to bake and to eat.

D is for Dear Daniel.

E is for earmuffs.

A stylish accessory for cold weather.

F is for friends.

What would you do without them?

G is for guitar.

Turn it up!

H is for hairstyles.

There's always something new to try.

I is for ice-skating.

I don't wobble any more, or not much, anyway!

J is for juice.

JUICE

How can anything this delicious be good for you? But it is!

K is for kawaii.

It's the Japanese word for cute, and describes me to a T.

L is for letters.

to Hello Kitty

Who knows what'll be in them?

M is for Mimmy.

My lovely twin.

N is for nice.

I have to admit it, I adore being nice, especially to my friends and my family.

O is for offcuts.

I love looking in the off-cuts section of the fabric shop. The odds and ends are so cheap, and who knows what you'll find?

P is for painting.

One of my favourite creative things to do.

Q is for quilt.

All snuggly and warm.

R is for rainbows.

S is for slippers.

So cute and so comfy!

T is for Teddy.

He doesn't talk much, but he's my oldest friend.

U is for USA.

I ♥ NY

One of my favourite holiday destinations.

V is for vintage.

One of my favourite style choices.

W is for wings.

The sparklier the better.

X is for xcuse.

It's so hard to think of something that genuinely begins with X, that I always have to xcuse myself!

Y is for yes.

I try to say yes to as many new experiences as possible, because you only live once!

Z is for zoo.

I love going to see all the different animals.

SCHOOL BUS

BUS STOP

47

Creative costuming

I love costume parties, and getting ready for them is half the fun. You can spend weeks planning a really elaborate costume, or throw something together in half an hour for that last-minute invitation. Here are some of my favourite easy-to-make costumes. Younger Hello Kitty fans should ask a grown-up for help with making costumes.

Wicked Witch

1. Make a pointy hat out of cardboard rolled into a funnel and glued or stapled together.
2. Streak your hair with grey temporary dye, or rub in talcum powder.
3. Make yourself a witchy nose by moulding a nose shape out of aluminium foil, covering it with masking tape then painting it green. Staple an elastic band to the nose so you can secure it around the back of your head.
4. Use a black eyeliner pencil to draw big moles on your face. If you want to black out one or two of your teeth, you can get special cosmetics from costume shops.
5. Dig out your oldest black clothes or take a trip to the charity shop - several skirts worn together produces the best effect, topped off with sweaters that have holes in.
6. Select an old black skirt and cut it up the middle to make a cape, which you can pin round your neck.
7. Black shoes and a broomstick complete the look!

Fluttery Fairy

1. Find a long T-shirt and cut the bottom hem in a zigzag pattern. Pink is best, but fairies can be any colour.
2. Add brightly coloured tights or leggings, along with ballet shoes, slippers or sandals.
3. Sew or stick in as many ribbons, leaves, feathers and glitter as you like.
4. Make a fairy headdress by attaching flowers to a headband. You could also tuck flowers behind your ears, or draw them on your face with washable pen.
5. Take a chopstick or other piece of sanded-down wood and cover it with silver foil to make a wand. For the perfect magical finish, cut out a silver star to stick on the tip!

Perilous Pirate

1. Pirates wore knee breeches, which are hard to get these days. Instead, squeeze into an outgrown pair of trousers, and pull them up so the cuffs sit just below your knees.
2. Knee-high leather boots with buckles are best for the pirate look, but failing that black loafers will also work.
3. A long velvet frock coat would be fantastic for a pirate costume, but probably difficult to find. Try wearing a velvet shirt open at the front - if you get an oversized one at a charity shop, it should be jacket-sized. Another option for a top is the traditional blue - or red-and-white striped jersey.
4. If you want a tricorn hat you may have to buy it, but plenty of pirates just wore a brightly-coloured kerchief on their heads.
5. Top it all off with as much jewellery as you can, especially gold hoop earrings. Pirates love bling!
6. Finally don't forget the tools of a pirate's trade - time to raid your little brother's room for his toy swords and knives.

You can dress up as just about anything, even if you're not into clothes. Dear Daniel once cut the centre out of a cardboard box, drew a bowl on the front and went to a party as a box of cereal!

Chinese horoscopes

My birthday is 1 November, which makes me a Scorpio in the Western horoscope system. But according to the Chinese system, which goes by the year you were born instead of the month, I'm a Tiger!

What's your Chinese star sign?

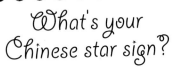

1980 Year of the Monkey
1981 Year of the Rooster
1982 Year of the Dog
1983 Year of the Boar
1984 Year of the Rat
1985 Year of the Ox
1986 Year of the Tiger
1987 Year of the Rabbit
1988 Year of the Dragon
1989 Year of the Snake
1990 Year of the Horse
1991 Year of the Ram
1992 Year of the Monkey
1993 Year of the Rooster
1994 Year of the Dog
1995 Year of the Boar
1996 Year of the Rat
1997 Year of the Ox
1998 Year of the Tiger
1999 Year of the Rabbit
2000 Year of the Dragon
2001 Year of the Snake
2002 Year of the Horse
2003 Year of the Ram
2004 Year of the Monkey
2005 Year of the Rooster
2006 Year of the Dog
2007 Year of the Boar
2008 Year of the Rat
2009 Year of the Ox
2010 Year of the Tiger
2011 Year of the Rabbit

Dog
People born in the year of the Dog are considered to be loyal, honest and reliable. However this can turn into a tendency to worry and find fault. They are industrious, and make good friends.

Boar
The Chinese don't regard pigs as dirty but scrupulous and sincere. People born in the Year of the Boar are lucky and likely to be successful in both business and academic studies.

Rat
The rat is considered a symbol of good luck and wealth in the far East. People born in Rat years are charming, inventive and generous, but they can also be short-tempered and picky.

Ox
Ox people are patient, and inspire the confidence of others. They are good with their hands and very methodical. On the downside they can be conservative and take a plodding approach to life.

Tiger
I like being a Tiger! We're born leaders, and good at fighting our corners. Less good is the Tiger's tendency to get carried away with her own ideas. I don't do that - do I?

Rabbit

Rabbit people like to socialise, and are good at smoothing over confrontation. Other people like to be around them, but they can sometimes be too shy.

Dragon

The Dragon is one of the luckiest and most powerful signs in the Chinese zodiac. Dragons are extroverts, who give great advice and have an eye for the latest trends. They can be stubborn if they don't get their own way.

Snake

Snakes are deep thinkers, as well as being romantic, charming and sympathetic. They strive for success, and can be self-critical and a bit stingy.

Horse

People born in the year of the horse are hard workers with a good grasp of money matters. They like to roam and may have a simultaneous yearning for independence and security.

Ram

Rams enjoy daydreaming, and are often known for their wisdom and gentleness. They sometimes limit themselves by being over-anxious, but often excel in the arts.

Monkey

Monkey people have magnetic personalities, but can be opportunistic. They are intelligent and vivacious, and crave activity and fun. At the same time, they are good listeners.

Rooster

Roosters are often eccentric types who like to dress flashily and show off. They think quickly, and are hard to fool. They have a particular love of honesty in themselves and other people.

Style update

Everyone has their comfort zone when it comes to clothes, but it's important to experiment too. As well as my favourite dresses, I like to experiment with all sorts of different looks. Trying new styles is a great way to brighten up a dull afternoon.

Here are some of my most daring styles. Why not give them a try yourself?

Retro Returns

Have you always wanted to be a flapper or a grand dame? Thanks to affordable modern materials, you can be a beauty from any era you like. If you're feeling really daring, why not blend your decades and try, for example, a full-skirted '50s dress with '70s punk accessories? Mix it up!

Go Goth

Black is so versatile, and it suits almost everyone. You can go for a plain black outfit that just hints at Goth style, or really get into it with accessories like fishnet gloves and leather. If you want a style that's both daring and feminine, add some wings for the gothic fairy look.

Cowgirl Cool

Yee-ha! A ten-gallon hat and riding boots will have heads a-turnin' as you stride down the street. Or if you don't want to go for the full on Wild West look, try mixing and matching individual elements, like a neckerchief with a rodeo-style denim skirt.

52

Get Up to Tweed

Tweed doesn't have to be boring. If you mix it with up-to-date accessories, it can create a striking, modern look.

Flower Girl

This one's great for summer. Start with a simple skirt and top, and then just twine in as many flowers as you can! Put them in your hair, behind your ears, around your buttons and pinned to your shirt.

Punk

If you've got attitude, show it by wearing spikes! You don't have to choose between looking streetwise or looking girly if you dress as a pretty pink punk.

Military

The military look is really in right now. Adding one or two core pieces of military clothing to your wardrobe will really give you an edge. Try a military jacket or coat in an army green, some khaki shorts or a funky belt with a military buckle.

Present picking

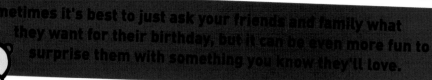

Sometimes it's best to just ask your friends and family what they want for their birthday, but it can be even more fun to surprise them with something you know they'll love.

Friends

Usually you will know your friends' tastes, and you may even have the perfect CD, book or accessory in mind before you start shopping. Make sure your choice of present isn't so obvious that they will get the same thing from someone else though.

★ Clothes are always a great choice, but you need to be sure that your gift will fit. Remember to keep the receipt, and try if possible to pick something that isn't too precisely fitted, rather than a shirt that might have the right size label but be the wrong shape for your friend.

★ If you're on a budget, a cute scarf or accessory can be an affordable option. If it's elegant and well-chosen, the price doesn't matter!

★ A present that celebrates your friendship can be really special, and also inexpensive if you're on a budget. I love to make pretty frames for special photos of fun things we've done together.

★ Event tickets are a good choice for friends who are into sport or music. Alternatively you could buy advance tickets for you both to visit a theme park. If money's tight, a birthday party in the park with a homemade picnic can be just as special. Don't forget to take your camera!

Other relatives

I never resort to bath oils. Even if you know very little about someone, some presents are much better to receive than others.

★ Almost everyone likes chocolates, and if they don't they will easily be able to find someone else who will enjoy them!

★ You can buy gift cards for things like books and CDs, or if you really know nothing about the recipient, you could get them gift cards for a department store or online shop which sells lots of different things.

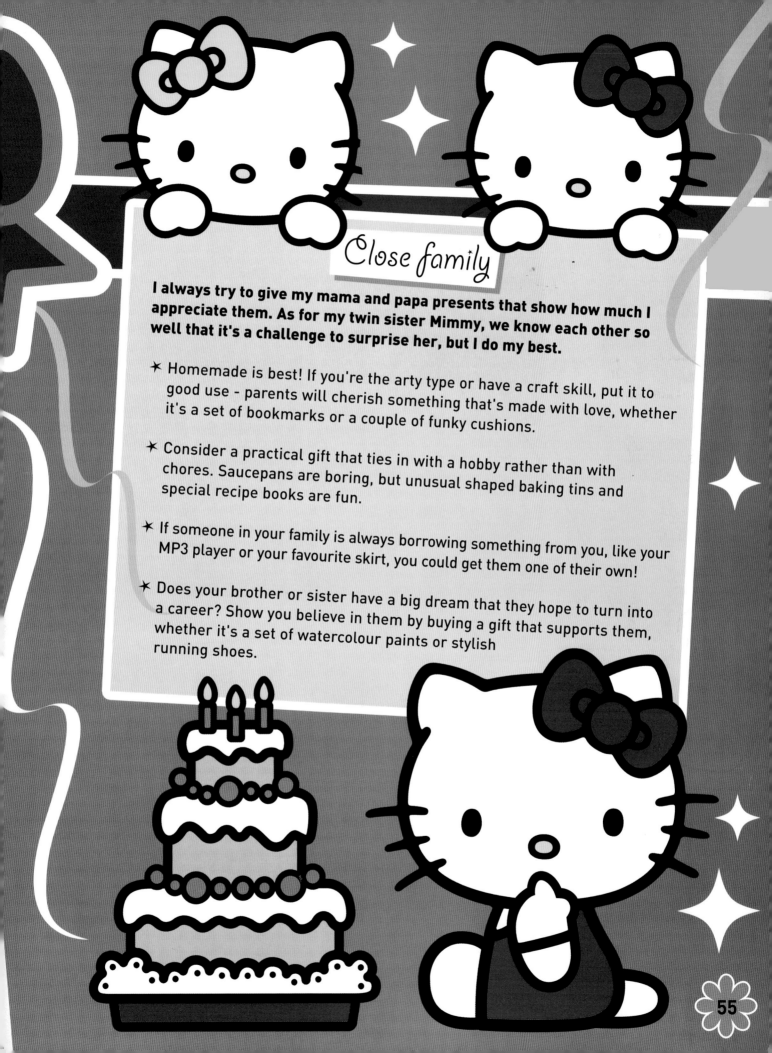

Close family

I always try to give my mama and papa presents that show how much I appreciate them. As for my twin sister Mimmy, we know each other so well that it's a challenge to surprise her, but I do my best.

★ Homemade is best! If you're the arty type or have a craft skill, put it to good use - parents will cherish something that's made with love, whether it's a set of bookmarks or a couple of funky cushions.

★ Consider a practical gift that ties in with a hobby rather than with chores. Saucepans are boring, but unusual shaped baking tins and special recipe books are fun.

★ If someone in your family is always borrowing something from you, like your MP3 player or your favourite skirt, you could get them one of their own!

★ Does your brother or sister have a big dream that they hope to turn into a career? Show you believe in them by buying a gift that supports them, whether it's a set of watercolour paints or stylish running shoes.

Party time

Around holiday times, it's great to have a party. You can host a small gathering for friends, or if you have a large extended family you might find yourself entertaining relatives you don't know very well. Either way these tips will help your evening go with the right kind of bang.

Food

* Plan your menu in advance, taking note of the likes and dislikes of your guests, and try to provide vegetarian options too if you're serving meat or fish. If you don't know, make sure to include plenty of classics such as garlic bread and dips.

* Unless you are preparing a sit-down dinner, go for bite-sized food. Nobody wants to eat spaghetti bolognese standing up!

* Get plenty of provisions in but take care not to overstuff your fridge. If cold air can't circulate properly, the food will spoil.

* It's a good idea to buy disposable plates and cutlery, just in case your ordinary crockery runs out. Plus, it saves on the washing-up, and you can recycle them.

Decorations

★ Try making imaginative centrepieces and ornaments, such as a pile of fruit decorated with tinsel and baubles.
★ How much of the house are you using for the party? Make sure that your guests will fit comfortably in the available space. If your friends are lively, consider locking everything breakable in a spare bedroom.

Entertainment

★ If you have room, and your neighbours won't mind, consider live music. If any of your friends are in a band, they'd surely love to play a set on the night. You can always invite your neighbours to join in!
★ You could make your party a fancy dress event, or give it a theme such as the 1960s.

Guests

★ If it's a family event, there will most likely be young children present, so remember to have plenty of fun stuff to keep them entertained.
★ A good way to keep everyone entertained (and guaranteed to turn up) is by organising a Secret Santa: ask everyone to pick a name from a hat, and to buy a gift for that person. But remember to keep it a secret!
★ Try to invite people as far in advance as possible, as the holidays are a busy time in everyone's social calendar.

All about me

Name: *Amelia*
Age: *8*
Star sign: ....
Email address: ....
....
Where I live: *I live in*
London Se greenwich
....
....

Stick a photo of yourself here!

Hobbies:
Sport
Dancing
Singing

My Favourites...

My best friend is called: ....
...... *Robert Wright* ....

My favourite music: ....
JD
Pop
....

My favourite films: ....
Scary
Sad
Love
....

My favourite sports:
Swimming, tennis
My favourite sweet treats: *Chocolate*
cakes ice-cream ....

My favourite holiday:

Use this space to write memories of your travels, and stick in photos, postcards, plane tickets, or anything else you can think of that reminds you of your trip!

....
....
....
....
....
....
....
....
....
....
....
....
....
....
....
....
....
....
....
....
....
....

Attach a snap of the two of you having fun together!

My favourite shoes. Aren't they cute?

Fashion Favourites...

My favourite shop: ....
My favourite style: ....
....
....
My favourite outfit: ....
....

This is me looking just fabulous in my favourite outfit!

My favourite designer: ....
My favourite colour: ....
My favourite shoes: ....
My favourite fashionista: ....

Goodbye!

I hope you've enjoyed my annual, and that it's given you plenty of top ideas for the year ahead! Make sure you fill your year with the things you love the most, like I do, and remember to try some new experiences too.

If you're ever stuck for things to do, and need activity ideas, you'll know where to look!

Lots of love,

Hello Kitty
x x

100+248=348

H	T	u
1	0	0
2	4	8
3	4	8

193+733=826

H	T	u
1	9	3
7	3	3

Th	H	T	u
2	6	4	8
4	3	6	4
1	1		1
8	1	6	2
1	6		

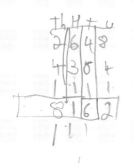

1